NAME

_____

TO

_____

DATE

_____

No.	Book Title	Your Book Genres						
		Classic	Crime					

No.	Book Title	Your Book Genres						
		Classic	Crime					

No.	Book Title	Your Book Genres						
		Classic	Crime					

No.	Book Title	Your Book Genres						
		Classic	Crime					

Book Title:

No.

Author: _____

Publisher: _____

Pages: _____

Book Genre: _____
_____

Started Date

_____

Finished Date

_____

My Review: _____

_____

_____

_____

_____

_____

_____

_____

_____

_____

_____

_____

_____

_____

My Inspiration

_____

_____

_____

_____

_____

_____

_____

My Rating

_____

_____

_____

_____

_____

_____

Take Notes:

Book Title:

No.

Author: _____

Publisher: _____

Pages: _____

Book Genre: _____

_____

My Review: _____

_____

_____

_____

_____

_____

_____

_____

_____

_____

_____

_____

_____

Take Notes:

Started Date

_____

Finished Date

_____

My Inspiration

_____

_____

_____

_____

_____

_____

My Rating

_____

_____

_____

_____

_____

Book Title:

No.

Author: _____

Publisher: _____

Pages: _____

Book Genre: _____

_____

My Review: _____

_____

_____

_____

_____

_____

_____

_____

_____

_____

_____

_____

_____

Take Notes:

Started Date

_____

Finished Date

_____

My Inspiration

_____

_____

_____

_____

_____

_____

My Rating

_____

_____

_____

_____

_____

Book Title:

No.

Author: _____

Publisher: _____

Pages: _____

Book Genre: _____

_____

My Review: _____

_____
_____
_____
_____
_____
_____
_____
_____
_____
_____
_____
_____

Take Notes:

Started Date
_____

Finished Date
_____

My Inspiration
_____
_____
_____
_____
_____
_____

My Rating
_____
_____
_____
_____
_____

Book Title:

No.

Author: _____

Publisher: _____

Pages: _____

Book Genre: _____

_____

Started Date

_____

Finished Date

_____

My Review: _____

_____

_____

_____

_____

_____

_____

_____

_____

_____

_____

_____

_____

_____

My Inspiration

_____

_____

_____

_____

_____

_____

_____

My Rating

_____

_____

_____

Take Notes:

_____

_____

_____

_____

Book Title:

No.

Author: _____

Started Date
_____

Publisher: _____

Pages: _____

Finished Date
_____

Book Genre: _____

_____

My Review: _____

My Inspiration

_____

_____

_____

_____

_____

_____

_____

_____

_____

My Rating

_____

_____

_____

_____

Take Notes:

_____

_____

Book Title:

No.

Author: _____

Publisher: _____

Pages: _____

Book Genre: _____
_____

Started Date
_____

Finished Date
_____

My Review: _____
_____
_____
_____
_____
_____
_____
_____
_____
_____
_____
_____
_____
_____

My Inspiration
_____
_____
_____
_____
_____
_____

My Rating

_____
_____
_____
_____
_____
_____

Take Notes:

Book Title:

No.

Author: _____

Publisher: _____

Pages: _____

Book Genre: _____

_____

Started Date

_____

Finished Date

_____

My Review: _____

_____

_____

_____

_____

_____

_____

_____

_____

_____

_____

_____

_____

My Inspiration

_____

_____

_____

_____

_____

My Rating

Take Notes:

_____

_____

_____

_____

_____

Book Title:

No.

Author: _____

Publisher: _____

Pages: _____

Book Genre: _____
_____

My Review: _____
_____
_____
_____
_____
_____
_____
_____
_____
_____
_____
_____
_____
_____
_____

Take Notes:

Started Date
_____

Finished Date
_____

My Inspiration
_____
_____
_____
_____
_____
_____

My Rating

_____
_____
_____
_____
_____

Book Title:

No.

Author: _____

Publisher: _____

Pages: _____

Book Genre: _____

_____

My Review: _____

_____

_____

_____

_____

_____

_____

_____

_____

_____

_____

_____

_____

_____

Take Notes:

Started Date

_____

Finished Date

_____

My Inspiration

_____

_____

_____

_____

_____

_____

My Rating

_____

_____

_____

_____

Book Title:

No.

Author: _____

Publisher: _____

Pages: _____

Book Genre: _____

_____

Started Date
_____

Finished Date
_____

My Review: _____

_____

_____

_____

_____

_____

_____

_____

_____

_____

_____

_____

_____

_____

My Inspiration
_____

_____

_____

_____

_____

_____

My Rating

_____

_____

Take Notes:

_____

_____

_____

_____

Book Title:

No.

Author: _____

Publisher: _____

Pages: _____

Book Genre: _____

_____

My Review: _____

_____

_____

_____

_____

_____

_____

_____

_____

_____

_____

_____

_____

Take Notes:

Started Date

_____

Finished Date

_____

My Inspiration

_____

_____

_____

_____

_____

_____

My Rating

_____

_____

_____

_____

_____

_____

Book Title:

No.

Author: _____

Publisher: _____

Pages: _____

Book Genre: _____

_____

My Review: _____

_____

_____

_____

_____

_____

_____

_____

_____

_____

_____

_____

_____

Take Notes:

Started Date
_____

Finished Date
_____

My Inspiration

_____

_____

_____

_____

_____

_____

My Rating

_____

_____

_____

_____

_____

Book Title:

No.

Author: _____

Started Date
_____

Publisher: _____

Pages: _____

Finished Date
_____

Book Genre: _____
_____

My Review: _____

My Inspiration
_____
_____
_____
_____
_____
_____

My Rating

_____

Take Notes:

_____
_____
_____
_____

Book Title:

No.

Author: _____

Publisher: _____

Pages: _____

Book Genre: _____

_____

Started Date

_____

Finished Date

_____

My Review: _____

_____

_____

_____

_____

_____

_____

_____

_____

_____

_____

_____

_____

_____

My Inspiration

_____

_____

_____

_____

_____

_____

_____

My Rating

_____

_____

_____

_____

_____

Take Notes:

Book Title:

No.

Author: _____

Publisher: _____

Pages: _____

Book Genre: _____
_____

My Review: _____
_____
_____
_____
_____
_____
_____
_____
_____
_____
_____
_____
_____
_____
_____

Take Notes:

Started Date
_____

Finished Date
_____

My Inspiration
_____
_____
_____
_____
_____
_____

My Rating

_____
_____
_____
_____
_____

Book Title:

No.

Author: _____

Publisher: _____

Pages: _____

Book Genre: _____

_____

Started Date

_____

Finished Date

_____

My Review: _____

_____

_____

_____

_____

_____

_____

_____

_____

_____

_____

_____

_____

My Inspiration

_____

_____

_____

_____

_____

_____

My Rating

_____

_____

Take Notes:

_____

_____

_____

_____

Book Title:

No.

Author: _____

Publisher: _____

Pages: _____

Book Genre: _____

_____

Started Date

_____

Finished Date

_____

My Review: _____

_____

_____

_____

_____

_____

_____

_____

_____

_____

_____

_____

_____

My Inspiration

_____

_____

_____

_____

_____

_____

My Rating

Take Notes:

_____

_____

_____

_____

_____

_____

Book Title:

No.

Author: _____

Publisher: _____

Pages: _____

Book Genre: _____

_____

Started Date

_____

Finished Date

_____

My Review: _____

_____

_____

_____

_____

_____

_____

_____

_____

_____

_____

_____

_____

_____

My Inspiration

_____

_____

_____

_____

_____

_____

My Rating

_____

Take Notes:

_____

_____

_____

_____

Book Title:

No.

Author: _____

Publisher: _____

Pages: _____

Book Genre: _____

_____

Started Date

_____

Finished Date

_____

My Review: _____

_____

_____

_____

_____

_____

_____

_____

_____

_____

_____

_____

_____

My Inspiration

_____

_____

_____

_____

_____

_____

My Rating

_____

Take Notes:

_____

_____

_____

_____

Book Title:

No.

Author: _____

Publisher: _____

Pages: _____

Book Genre: _____

_____

Started Date

_____

Finished Date

_____

My Review: _____

_____

_____

_____

_____

_____

_____

_____

_____

_____

_____

_____

_____

My Inspiration

_____

_____

_____

_____

_____

_____

My Rating

Take Notes:

_____

_____

_____

_____

_____

_____

Book Title:

No.

Author: _____

Publisher: _____

Pages: _____

Book Genre: _____

_____

My Review: _____

_____

_____

_____

_____

_____

_____

_____

_____

_____

_____

_____

_____

Take Notes:

Started Date

_____

Finished Date

_____

My Inspiration

_____

_____

_____

_____

_____

My Rating

_____

_____

_____

_____

Book Title:

No.

Author: _____

Publisher: _____

Pages: _____

Book Genre: _____

_____

My Review: _____

_____

_____

_____

_____

_____

_____

_____

_____

_____

_____

_____

_____

Take Notes:

Started Date

_____

Finished Date

_____

My Inspiration

_____

_____

_____

_____

_____

_____

My Rating

_____

_____

_____

_____

_____

_____

Book Title:

No.

Author: _____

Publisher: _____

Pages: _____

Book Genre: _____

_____

My Review: _____

_____

_____

_____

_____

_____

_____

_____

_____

_____

_____

_____

_____

Take Notes:

Started Date

_____

Finished Date

_____

My Inspiration

_____

_____

_____

_____

_____

My Rating

_____

_____

_____

_____

Book Title:

No.

Author: _____

Started Date
_____

Publisher: _____

Pages: _____

Finished Date
_____

Book Genre: _____
_____

My Review: _____

My Inspiration

_____
_____
_____
_____
_____
_____
_____
_____
_____

_____
_____
_____
_____

My Rating

_____
_____

Take Notes:

_____
_____
_____
_____

Book Title:

No.

Author: _____

Publisher: _____

Pages: _____

Book Genre: _____

_____

Started Date

_____

Finished Date

_____

My Review: _____

_____

_____

_____

_____

_____

_____

_____

_____

_____

_____

_____

_____

My Inspiration

_____

_____

_____

_____

_____

_____

My Rating

_____

_____

Take Notes:

_____

_____

_____

Book Title:

No.

Author: _____

Publisher: _____

Pages: _____

Book Genre: _____

_____

My Review: _____

_____

_____

_____

_____

_____

_____

_____

_____

_____

_____

_____

_____

Take Notes:

Started Date
_____

Finished Date
_____

My Inspiration
_____

_____

_____

_____

_____

_____

_____

My Rating

_____

_____

_____

_____

_____

_____

Book Title:

No.

Author: _____

Publisher: _____

Pages: _____

Book Genre: _____

_____

My Review: _____

_____

_____

_____

_____

_____

_____

_____

_____

_____

_____

_____

Take Notes:

Started Date

_____

Finished Date

_____

My Inspiration

_____

_____

_____

_____

_____

My Rating

_____

_____

_____

_____

Book Title:

No.

Author: _____

Publisher: _____

Pages: _____

Book Genre: _____

_____

Started Date

_____

Finished Date

_____

My Review: _____

_____

_____

_____

_____

_____

_____

_____

_____

_____

_____

_____

_____

_____

My Inspiration

_____

_____

_____

_____

_____

_____

My Rating

Take Notes:

_____

_____

_____

_____

_____

_____

Book Title:

No.

Author: _____
Publisher: _____
Pages: _____
Book Genre: _____
_____

Started Date
_____

Finished Date
_____

My Review: _____
_____
_____
_____
_____
_____
_____
_____
_____
_____
_____
_____
_____

My Inspiration
_____
_____
_____
_____
_____
_____

My Rating

_____
_____
_____
_____
_____

Take Notes:

Book Title:

No.

Author: _____

Publisher: _____

Pages: _____

Book Genre: _____

_____

My Review: _____

_____
_____
_____
_____
_____
_____
_____
_____
_____
_____
_____
_____
_____

Take Notes:

Started Date
_____

Finished Date
_____

My Inspiration

_____
_____
_____
_____
_____
_____

My Rating

_____
_____
_____
_____
_____

Book Title:

No.

Author: _____

Publisher: _____

Pages: _____

Book Genre: _____

_____

Started Date

_____

Finished Date

_____

My Review: _____

_____

_____

_____

_____

_____

_____

_____

_____

_____

_____

_____

_____

_____

My Inspiration

_____

_____

_____

_____

_____

_____

My Rating

_____

_____

Take Notes:

_____

_____

_____

_____

_____

Book Title:

No.

Author: _____

Publisher: _____

Pages: _____

Book Genre: _____

_____

Started Date

_____

Finished Date

_____

My Review: _____

_____

_____

_____

_____

_____

_____

_____

_____

_____

_____

_____

_____

_____

My Inspiration

_____

_____

_____

_____

_____

_____

My Rating

_____

_____

Take Notes:

_____

_____

_____

_____

Book Title:

No.

Author: _____

Started Date
_____

Publisher: _____

Finished Date
_____

Pages: _____

Book Genre: _____
_____

My Review: _____

My Inspiration
_____
_____
_____
_____
_____
_____
_____
_____
_____
_____
_____
_____
_____

My Rating
_____
_____
_____
_____

Take Notes:
_____
_____
_____
_____

Book Title:

No.

Author: _____

Publisher: _____

Pages: _____

Book Genre: _____

_____

My Review: _____

_____

_____

_____

_____

_____

_____

_____

_____

_____

_____

_____

_____

Take Notes:

Started Date
_____

Finished Date
_____

My Inspiration
_____
_____
_____
_____
_____
_____

My Rating

_____
_____
_____
_____
_____
_____

Book Title:

No.

Author: _____

Publisher: _____

Pages: _____

Book Genre: _____

_____

My Review: _____

_____

_____

_____

_____

_____

_____

_____

_____

_____

_____

_____

_____

Take Notes:

Started Date

_____

Finished Date

_____

My Inspiration

_____

_____

_____

_____

_____

_____

My Rating

_____

_____

_____

_____

_____

Book Title:

No.

Author: _____

Publisher: _____

Pages: _____

Book Genre: _____

_____

My Review: _____

_____

_____

_____

_____

_____

_____

_____

_____

_____

_____

_____

_____

Take Notes:

Started Date
_____

Finished Date
_____

My Inspiration

_____

_____

_____

_____

_____

_____

_____

My Rating

_____

_____

_____

_____

_____

_____

Book Title:

No.

Author: _____
Publisher: _____
Pages: _____
Book Genre: _____
_____

Started Date
_____

Finished Date
_____

My Review: _____
_____
_____
_____
_____
_____
_____
_____
_____
_____
_____
_____

My Inspiration
_____
_____
_____
_____
_____
_____

My Rating

_____
_____
_____
_____
_____

Take Notes:

Book Title:

No.

Author: _____

Publisher: _____

Pages: _____

Book Genre: _____

_____

My Review: _____

_____
_____
_____
_____
_____
_____
_____
_____
_____
_____
_____
_____
_____

Take Notes:

Started Date
_____

Finished Date
_____

My Inspiration
_____
_____
_____
_____
_____
_____

My Rating

_____
_____
_____
_____
_____
_____

Book Title:

No.

Author: _____

Publisher: _____

Pages: _____

Book Genre: _____

_____

Started Date

_____

Finished Date

_____

My Review: _____

_____

_____

_____

_____

_____

My Inspiration

_____

_____

_____

_____

_____

_____

_____

_____

_____

My Rating

_____

_____

_____

Take Notes:

_____

_____

_____

_____

_____

Book Title:

No.

Author: _____

Publisher: _____

Pages: _____

Book Genre: _____

_____

Started Date

_____

Finished Date

_____

My Review: _____

_____

_____

_____

_____

My Inspiration

_____

_____

_____

_____

_____

_____

_____

My Rating

_____

_____

_____

Take Notes:

_____

_____

_____

_____

Book Title:

No.

Author: _____

Started Date
_____

Publisher: _____

Pages: _____

Finished Date
_____

Book Genre: _____

_____

My Review: _____

My Inspiration

_____

_____

_____

_____

_____

_____

_____

_____

_____

My Rating

_____

_____

_____

Take Notes:

_____

_____

_____

_____

Book Title:

No.

Author: _____

Publisher: _____

Pages: _____

Book Genre: _____

_____

My Review: _____

_____
_____
_____
_____
_____
_____
_____
_____
_____
_____
_____

Take Notes:

Started Date

_____

Finished Date

_____

My Inspiration

_____
_____
_____
_____
_____
_____

My Rating

_____
_____
_____
_____
_____
_____

Book Title: No.

Author: _____   Started Date
Publisher: _____   _____
Pages: _____   Finished Date
Book Genre: _____   _____
_____

My Review: _____   My Inspiration
_____   _____
_____   _____
_____   _____
_____
_____   _____
_____   _____
_____
_____   _____
_____   _____
_____
_____   My Rating
_____
_____   _____
_____   _____

Take Notes: _____
                                                          _____
                                                          _____
                                                          _____

Book Title:

No.

Author: _____

Publisher: _____

Pages: _____

Book Genre: _____

_____

Started Date

_____

Finished Date

_____

My Review: _____

_____

_____

_____

_____

_____

_____

_____

_____

_____

_____

_____

_____

_____

_____

My Inspiration

_____

_____

_____

_____

_____

_____

My Rating

_____

_____

_____

Take Notes:

_____

_____

_____

Book Title:

No.

Author: _____

Publisher: _____

Pages: _____

Book Genre: _____

_____

My Review: _____

_____

_____

_____

_____

_____

_____

_____

_____

_____

_____

_____

_____

_____

_____

Take Notes:

Started Date

_____

Finished Date

_____

My Inspiration

_____

_____

_____

_____

_____

_____

My Rating

_____

_____

_____

_____

_____

Book Title:

No.

Author: _____

Publisher: _____

Pages: _____

Book Genre: _____

_____

Started Date
_____

Finished Date
_____

My Review: _____

_____

_____

_____

_____

_____

_____

_____

_____

_____

_____

_____

_____

My Inspiration
_____

_____

_____

_____

_____

_____

_____

My Rating

_____

_____

_____

_____

Take Notes:

Book Title:

No.

Author: _____
Publisher: _____
Pages: _____
Book Genre: _____
_____

My Review: _____
_____
_____
_____
_____
_____
_____
_____
_____
_____
_____
_____
_____

Take Notes:

Started Date
_____

Finished Date
_____

My Inspiration
_____
_____
_____
_____
_____
_____

My Rating
_____
_____
_____
_____
_____

Book Title:

No.

Author: _____

Publisher: _____

Pages: _____

Book Genre: _____

_____

My Review: _____

_____

_____

_____

_____

_____

_____

_____

_____

_____

_____

_____

_____

Take Notes:

Started Date
_____

Finished Date
_____

My Inspiration
_____

_____

_____

_____

_____

_____

My Rating
_____

_____

_____

_____

Book Title:

No.

Author: _____

Started Date
_____

Publisher: _____

Pages: _____

Finished Date
_____

Book Genre: _____
_____

My Review: _____

My Inspiration

_____
_____
_____
_____
_____
_____
_____
_____
_____

My Rating

_____
_____
_____
_____

Take Notes:

_____
_____
_____
_____
_____

Book Title:

No.

Author: _____

Publisher: _____

Pages: _____

Book Genre: _____

_____

My Review: _____

_____

_____

_____

_____

_____

_____

_____

_____

_____

_____

_____

_____

_____

_____

Take Notes:

Started Date

_____

Finished Date

_____

My Inspiration

_____

_____

_____

_____

_____

_____

My Rating

_____

_____

_____

_____

_____

_____

Book Title:

No.

Author: _____

Publisher: _____

Pages: _____

Book Genre: _____
_____

Started Date
_____

Finished Date
_____

My Review: _____
_____
_____
_____
_____
_____
_____
_____
_____
_____
_____
_____
_____
_____

My Inspiration
_____
_____
_____
_____
_____
_____

My Rating

Take Notes:

_____
_____
_____
_____
_____

Book Title:

No.

Author: _____

Publisher: _____

Pages: _____

Book Genre: _____

_____

My Review: _____

_____

_____

_____

_____

_____

_____

_____

_____

_____

_____

_____

_____

Take Notes:

Started Date

_____

Finished Date

_____

My Inspiration

_____

_____

_____

_____

_____

_____

_____

My Rating

_____

_____

_____

_____

_____

_____

Book Title:

No.

Author: _____

Publisher: _____

Pages: _____

Book Genre: _____

_____

My Review: _____

_____

_____

_____

_____

_____

_____

_____

_____

_____

_____

_____

Take Notes:

Started Date
_____

Finished Date
_____

My Inspiration
_____

_____

_____

_____

_____

My Rating

_____

_____

_____

_____

Book Title:

No.

Author: _____

Publisher: _____

Pages: _____

Book Genre: _____

_____

My Review: _____

_____

_____

_____

_____

_____

_____

_____

_____

_____

_____

_____

_____

_____

Take Notes:

Started Date

_____

Finished Date

_____

My Inspiration

_____

_____

_____

_____

_____

_____

_____

My Rating

_____

_____

_____

_____

_____

Book Title:

No.

Author: _____

Publisher: _____

Pages: _____

Book Genre: _____

_____

Started Date
_____

Finished Date
_____

My Review: _____

_____

_____

_____

_____

_____

_____

_____

_____

_____

_____

_____

_____

_____

My Inspiration
_____
_____
_____
_____
_____
_____

My Rating

_____
_____
_____
_____
_____

Take Notes:

Book Title:

No.

Author: _____

Publisher: _____

Pages: _____

Book Genre: _____

_____

My Review: _____

_____

_____

_____

_____

_____

_____

_____

_____

_____

_____

_____

_____

Take Notes:

Started Date

_____

Finished Date

_____

My Inspiration

_____

_____

_____

_____

_____

_____

_____

My Rating

_____

_____

_____

_____

_____

Book Title:

No.

Author: _____

Publisher: _____

Pages: _____

Book Genre: _____

_____

Started Date

_____

Finished Date

_____

My Review: _____

_____

_____

_____

_____

_____

_____

_____

_____

_____

_____

_____

_____

_____

My Inspiration

_____

_____

_____

_____

_____

_____

_____

My Rating

_____

_____

Take Notes:

_____

_____

_____

_____

Book Title:

No.

Author: _____

Publisher: _____

Pages: _____

Book Genre: _____

_____

Started Date

_____

Finished Date

_____

My Review: _____

_____

_____

_____

_____

_____

_____

_____

_____

_____

_____

_____

_____

_____

My Inspiration

_____

_____

_____

_____

_____

_____

_____

My Rating

Take Notes:

_____

_____

_____

_____

_____

_____

Book Title:

No.

Author: _____

Publisher: _____

Pages: _____

Book Genre: _____

_____

My Review: _____

_____

_____

_____

_____

_____

_____

_____

_____

_____

_____

_____

_____

_____

Take Notes:

Started Date

_____

Finished Date

_____

My Inspiration

_____

_____

_____

_____

_____

My Rating

_____

_____

_____

_____

_____

Book Title:

No.

Author: _____

Publisher: _____

Pages: _____

Book Genre: _____

_____

Started Date

_____

Finished Date

_____

My Review: _____

_____

_____

_____

_____

_____

_____

_____

_____

_____

_____

_____

_____

_____

My Inspiration

_____

_____

_____

_____

_____

_____

My Rating

_____

Take Notes:

_____

_____

_____

_____

_____

Book Title:

No.

Author: _____

Publisher: _____

Pages: _____

Book Genre: _____
_____

Started Date
_____

Finished Date
_____

My Review: _____
_____
_____
_____
_____
_____
_____
_____
_____
_____
_____
_____
_____

My Inspiration
_____
_____
_____
_____
_____
_____

My Rating
_____
_____
_____
_____
_____

Take Notes:

Book Title:

No.

Author: _____

Started Date
_____

Publisher: _____

Pages: _____

Finished Date
_____

Book Genre: _____
_____

My Review: _____

My Inspiration
_____
_____
_____
_____
_____
_____
_____
_____

_____
_____
_____
_____
_____
_____
_____
_____

My Rating

_____
_____
_____

Take Notes:

_____
_____
_____
_____
_____

Book Title:

No.

Author: _____

Publisher: _____

Pages: _____

Book Genre: _____

_____

My Review: _____

_____

_____

_____

_____

_____

_____

_____

_____

_____

_____

_____

Take Notes:

Started Date

_____

Finished Date

_____

My Inspiration

_____

_____

_____

_____

_____

_____

My Rating

_____

_____

_____

_____

Book Title:

No.

Author: _____

_____

Publisher: _____

Pages: _____

Finished Date
_____

Book Genre: _____

_____

My Review: _____

My Inspiration

_____

_____

_____

_____

_____

_____

_____

_____

_____

_____

_____

My Rating

_____

_____

_____

_____

Take Notes:

_____

_____

_____

_____

_____

_____

Book Title: No.

Author: _____   Started Date
Publisher: _____   _____
Pages: _____   Finished Date
Book Genre: _____   _____
_____

My Review: _____   My Inspiration
_____   _____
_____   _____
_____   _____
_____   _____
_____   _____
_____   _____
_____
_____   My Rating
_____
_____
_____   _____
_____   _____
Take Notes: _____
                                           _____
                                           _____

Book Title:

No.

Author: _____

Publisher: _____

Pages: _____

Book Genre: _____

_____

Started Date

_____

Finished Date

_____

My Review: _____

_____

_____

_____

_____

_____

_____

_____

_____

_____

_____

_____

_____

_____

My Inspiration

_____

_____

_____

_____

_____

_____

My Rating

_____

_____

_____

_____

Take Notes:

_____

_____

Book Title:

No.

Author: _____

Publisher: _____

Pages: _____

Book Genre: _____

_____

My Review: _____

_____
_____
_____
_____
_____
_____
_____
_____
_____
_____
_____
_____
_____

Take Notes:

Started Date
_____

Finished Date
_____

My Inspiration

_____
_____
_____
_____
_____

My Rating

_____
_____
_____
_____
_____

Book Title:

No.

Author: _____

Publisher: _____

Pages: _____

Book Genre: _____

_____

My Review: _____

_____
_____
_____
_____
_____
_____
_____
_____
_____
_____
_____
_____
_____

Take Notes:

Started Date

_____

Finished Date

_____

My Inspiration

_____
_____
_____
_____
_____
_____

My Rating

_____
_____
_____
_____
_____
_____

Book Title:

No.

Author: _____

Started Date
_____

Publisher: _____

Pages: _____

Finished Date
_____

Book Genre: _____

_____

My Review: _____

My Inspiration

_____

_____

_____

_____

_____

_____

_____

_____

_____

My Rating

_____

_____

_____

Take Notes:

_____

_____

_____

Book Title:

No.

Author: _____

Publisher: _____

Pages: _____

Book Genre: _____

_____

My Review: _____

_____

_____

_____

_____

_____

_____

_____

_____

_____

_____

_____

_____

_____

Take Notes:

Started Date

_____

Finished Date

_____

My Inspiration

_____

_____

_____

_____

_____

_____

My Rating

_____

_____

_____

_____

_____

Book Title:

No.

Author: _____

Publisher: _____

Pages: _____

Book Genre: _____

_____

My Review: _____

_____

_____

_____

_____

_____

_____

_____

_____

_____

_____

_____

_____

_____

Take Notes:

Started Date

_____

Finished Date

_____

My Inspiration

_____

_____

_____

_____

_____

_____

My Rating

_____

_____

_____

_____

_____

Book Title: _____ No.

Author: _____

Publisher: _____

Pages: _____

Book Genre: _____

_____

My Review: _____

_____

_____

_____

_____

_____

_____

_____

_____

_____

_____

_____

_____

Take Notes:

Started Date

_____

Finished Date

_____

My Inspiration

_____

_____

_____

_____

_____

_____

_____

My Rating

_____

_____

_____

_____

_____

_____

Book Title: No.

Author: _____ Started Date

Publisher: _____ _____

Pages: _____ Finished Date

Book Genre: _____ _____

_____

My Review: _____ My Inspiration

_____ _____

_____ _____

_____ _____

_____ _____

_____

_____ _____

_____ _____

_____

_____

_____ My Rating

_____

_____

_____

_____ _____

_____ _____

Take Notes: _____

_____

_____

_____

Book Title:

No.

Author: _____

Publisher: _____

Pages: _____

Book Genre: _____

_____

Started Date

_____

Finished Date

_____

My Review: _____

_____

_____

_____

_____

_____

_____

_____

_____

_____

_____

_____

_____

_____

My Inspiration

_____

_____

_____

_____

_____

_____

_____

My Rating

_____

_____

Take Notes:

_____

_____

_____

_____

Book Title:

No.

Author: _____

Started Date
_____

Publisher: _____

Pages: _____

Finished Date
_____

Book Genre: _____

_____

My Review: _____

_____
_____
_____
_____
_____
_____
_____
_____
_____
_____
_____
_____
_____
_____
_____

My Inspiration

_____
_____
_____
_____
_____

My Rating

_____
_____
_____
_____
_____

Take Notes:

Book Title:

No.

Author: _____

Publisher: _____

Pages: _____

Book Genre: _____

_____

My Review: _____

_____

_____

_____

_____

_____

_____

_____

_____

_____

_____

_____

_____

_____

Take Notes:

Started Date

_____

Finished Date

_____

My Inspiration

_____

_____

_____

_____

_____

_____

My Rating

_____

_____

_____

_____

_____

_____

Book Title:

No.

Author: _____
Publisher: _____
Pages: _____
Book Genre: _____
_____

Started Date
_____

Finished Date
_____

My Review: _____
_____
_____
_____
_____
_____
_____
_____
_____
_____
_____
_____
_____
_____

My Inspiration
_____
_____
_____
_____
_____
_____

My Rating

Take Notes:

_____
_____
_____
_____
_____

Book Title:

No.

Author: _____

Publisher: _____

Pages: _____

Book Genre: _____

_____

Started Date

_____

Finished Date

_____

My Review: _____

_____

_____

_____

_____

_____

_____

_____

_____

_____

_____

_____

_____

_____

_____

My Inspiration

_____

_____

_____

_____

_____

_____

My Rating

_____

_____

Take Notes:

_____

_____

_____

_____

Book Title:

No.

Author: _____

Publisher: _____

Pages: _____

Book Genre: _____

_____

My Review: _____

_____

_____

_____

_____

_____

_____

_____

_____

_____

_____

_____

_____

Take Notes:

Started Date

_____

Finished Date

_____

My Inspiration

_____

_____

_____

_____

_____

My Rating

_____

_____

_____

_____

Book Title:

No.

Author: _____

Publisher: _____

Pages: _____

Book Genre: _____

_____

My Review: _____

_____

_____

_____

_____

_____

_____

_____

_____

_____

_____

_____

_____

_____

Take Notes:

Started Date

_____

Finished Date

_____

My Inspiration

_____

_____

_____

_____

_____

_____

_____

My Rating

_____

_____

_____

_____

_____

_____

Book Title:

No.

Author: _____

Publisher: _____

Pages: _____

Book Genre: _____

_____

My Review: _____

_____
_____
_____
_____
_____
_____
_____
_____
_____
_____
_____
_____

Take Notes:

Started Date

_____

Finished Date

_____

My Inspiration

_____
_____
_____
_____
_____

My Rating

_____
_____
_____
_____
_____

Book Title:

No.

Author: _____

Publisher: _____

Pages: _____

Book Genre: _____

_____

My Review: _____

_____
_____
_____
_____
_____
_____
_____
_____
_____
_____
_____
_____
_____

Take Notes:

Started Date
_____

Finished Date
_____

My Inspiration

_____
_____
_____
_____
_____
_____

My Rating

_____
_____
_____
_____
_____
_____

Book Title:

No.

Author: _____

Started Date

Publisher: _____

_____

Pages: _____

Finished Date

Book Genre: _____

_____

_____

My Review: _____

My Inspiration

_____

_____

_____

_____

_____

_____

_____

_____

_____

_____

_____

_____

My Rating

_____

_____

_____

_____

_____

Take Notes:

_____

_____

_____

_____

Book Title:

No.

Author: _____

Publisher: _____

Pages: _____

Book Genre: _____

_____

Started Date

_____

Finished Date

_____

My Review: _____

_____

_____

_____

_____

_____

_____

_____

_____

_____

_____

_____

_____

_____

My Inspiration

_____

_____

_____

_____

_____

_____

_____

My Rating

_____

_____

Take Notes:

_____

_____

_____

_____

_____

Book Title:

No.

Author: _____

Publisher: _____

Pages: _____

Book Genre: _____

_____

My Review: _____

_____

_____

_____

_____

_____

_____

_____

_____

_____

_____

_____

_____

Take Notes:

Started Date

_____

Finished Date

_____

My Inspiration

_____

_____

_____

_____

_____

My Rating

_____

_____

_____

_____

Book Title:

No.

Author: _____

Publisher: _____

Pages: _____

Book Genre: _____

_____

Started Date

_____

Finished Date

_____

My Review: _____

_____

_____

_____

_____

_____

_____

_____

_____

_____

_____

_____

_____

_____

_____

My Inspiration

_____

_____

_____

_____

_____

_____

My Rating

_____

_____

_____

Take Notes:

_____

_____

Book Title:

No.

Author: _____

Publisher: _____

Pages: _____

Book Genre: _____

_____

My Review: _____

_____

_____

_____

_____

_____

_____

_____

_____

_____

_____

_____

_____

_____

Take Notes:

Started Date

_____

Finished Date

_____

My Inspiration

_____

_____

_____

_____

_____

My Rating

_____

_____

_____

_____

_____

Book Title:

No.

Author: _____

Publisher: _____

Pages: _____

Book Genre: _____

_____

My Review: _____

_____

_____

_____

_____

_____

_____

_____

_____

_____

_____

_____

_____

_____

Take Notes:

Started Date

_____

Finished Date

_____

My Inspiration

_____

_____

_____

_____

_____

_____

My Rating

_____

_____

_____

_____

_____

_____

Book Title:

No.

Author: _____

Publisher: _____

Pages: _____

Book Genre: _____
_____

Started Date
_____

Finished Date
_____

My Review: _____
_____
_____
_____
_____
_____
_____
_____
_____
_____
_____
_____
_____
_____

My Inspiration
_____
_____
_____
_____
_____

My Rating

_____
_____
_____
_____
_____

Take Notes:

Book Title:

No.

Author: _____

Publisher: _____

Pages: _____

Book Genre: _____

_____

Started Date

_____

Finished Date

_____

My Review: _____

_____

_____

_____

_____

_____

_____

_____

_____

_____

_____

_____

_____

My Inspiration

_____

_____

_____

_____

_____

_____

My Rating

Take Notes:

_____

_____

_____

_____

_____

Book Title:

No.

Author: _____
Publisher: _____
Pages: _____
Book Genre: _____
_____

Started Date
_____

Finished Date
_____

My Review: _____
_____
_____
_____
_____
_____
_____
_____
_____
_____
_____
_____
_____

My Inspiration
_____
_____
_____
_____
_____
_____

My Rating

_____
_____
_____
_____
_____

Take Notes:

Book Title:

No.

Author: _____

Publisher: _____

Pages: _____

Book Genre: _____

_____

My Review: _____

_____
_____
_____
_____
_____
_____
_____
_____
_____
_____
_____
_____

Take Notes:

Started Date

_____

Finished Date

_____

My Inspiration

_____
_____
_____
_____
_____
_____

My Rating

_____
_____
_____
_____
_____
_____

Book Title:

No.

Author: _____

Publisher: _____

Pages: _____

Book Genre: _____
_____

Started Date
_____

Finished Date
_____

My Review: _____
_____
_____
_____
_____
_____
_____
_____
_____
_____
_____
_____
_____
_____

My Inspiration
_____
_____
_____
_____
_____
_____

My Rating

Take Notes:

_____
_____
_____
_____
_____

Book Title:

No.

Author: _____

Publisher: _____

Pages: _____

Book Genre: _____

_____

Started Date

_____

Finished Date

_____

My Review: _____

_____
_____
_____
_____
_____
_____
_____
_____
_____
_____
_____
_____

My Inspiration

_____
_____
_____
_____
_____
_____

My Rating

Take Notes:

_____
_____
_____
_____
_____
_____

Book Title:

No.

Author: _____

Publisher: _____

Pages: _____

Book Genre: _____

_____

Started Date

_____

Finished Date

_____

My Review: _____

_____

_____

_____

_____

_____

_____

_____

_____

_____

_____

_____

My Inspiration

_____

_____

_____

_____

_____

My Rating

_____

_____

Take Notes:

_____

_____

_____

_____

Book Title:

No.

Author: _____

Publisher: _____

Pages: _____

Book Genre: _____
_____

Started Date
_____

Finished Date
_____

My Review: _____
_____
_____
_____
_____
_____
_____
_____
_____
_____
_____
_____
_____
_____

My Inspiration
_____
_____
_____
_____
_____
_____
_____

My Rating

Take Notes:

_____
_____
_____
_____
_____
_____

Book Title:

No.

Author: _____

Publisher: _____

Pages: _____

Book Genre: _____

_____

My Review: _____

_____

_____

_____

_____

_____

_____

_____

_____

_____

_____

_____

Take Notes:

Started Date
_____

Finished Date
_____

My Inspiration
_____
_____
_____
_____
_____
_____
_____

My Rating

_____
_____
_____
_____
_____

Book Title:

No.

Author: _____

Publisher: _____

Pages: _____

Book Genre: _____

_____

My Review: _____

_____

_____

_____

_____

_____

_____

_____

_____

_____

_____

_____

_____

Take Notes:

Started Date
_____

Finished Date
_____

My Inspiration
_____

_____

_____

_____

_____

_____

My Rating

_____

_____

_____

_____

_____

Book Title:

No.

Author: _____

Publisher: _____

Pages: _____

Book Genre: _____

_____

Started Date

_____

Finished Date

_____

My Review: _____

_____

_____

_____

_____

_____

_____

_____

_____

_____

_____

_____

_____

_____

My Inspiration

_____

_____

_____

_____

_____

_____

My Rating

_____

_____

_____

Take Notes:

_____

_____

_____

Book Title:

No.

Author: _____

Publisher: _____

Pages: _____

Book Genre: _____

_____

Started Date

_____

Finished Date

_____

My Review:

_____
_____
_____
_____
_____
_____
_____
_____
_____
_____
_____
_____
_____

My Inspiration

_____
_____
_____
_____
_____
_____
_____

My Rating

Take Notes:

_____
_____
_____
_____
_____
_____

Book Title:

No.

Author: _____

Publisher: _____

Pages: _____

Book Genre: _____

_____

Started Date

_____

Finished Date

_____

My Review: _____

_____

_____

_____

_____

_____

_____

_____

_____

_____

_____

_____

_____

_____

My Inspiration

_____

_____

_____

_____

_____

_____

My Rating

_____

Take Notes:

_____

_____

_____

_____

_____

Book Title:

No.

Author: _____

Publisher: _____

Pages: _____

Book Genre: _____

_____

My Review: _____

_____

_____

_____

_____

_____

_____

_____

_____

_____

_____

_____

_____

_____

Take Notes:

Started Date

_____

Finished Date

_____

My Inspiration

_____

_____

_____

_____

_____

_____

My Rating

_____

_____

_____

_____

_____

_____

Book Title:

No.

Author: _____

Publisher: _____

Pages: _____

Book Genre: _____

_____

My Review: _____

_____

_____

_____

_____

_____

_____

_____

_____

_____

_____

_____

_____

Take Notes:

Started Date

_____

Finished Date

_____

My Inspiration

_____

_____

_____

_____

_____

_____

My Rating

_____

_____

_____

_____

_____

Book Title:

No.

Author: _____

Publisher: _____

Pages: _____

Book Genre: _____

_____

Started Date

_____

Finished Date

_____

My Review: _____

_____

_____

_____

_____

_____

_____

_____

_____

_____

_____

_____

_____

_____

My Inspiration

_____

_____

_____

_____

_____

_____

_____

My Rating

_____

Take Notes:

_____

_____

_____

_____

Book Title:

No.

Author: _____

Publisher: _____

Pages: _____

Book Genre: _____

_____

My Review: _____

_____

_____

_____

_____

_____

_____

_____

_____

_____

_____

_____

Take Notes:

Started Date

_____

Finished Date

_____

My Inspiration

_____

_____

_____

_____

_____

_____

My Rating

_____

_____

_____

_____

_____

Book Title:

No.

Author: _____

Publisher: _____

Pages: _____

Book Genre: _____
_____

Started Date
_____

Finished Date
_____

My Review: _____
_____
_____
_____
_____
_____
_____
_____
_____
_____
_____
_____
_____

My Inspiration
_____
_____
_____
_____
_____
_____
_____

My Rating

Take Notes:

_____
_____
_____
_____
_____

Book Title:

No.

Author: _____

Publisher: _____

Pages: _____

Book Genre: _____

_____

My Review: _____

_____

_____

_____

_____

_____

_____

_____

_____

_____

_____

_____

_____

_____

_____

_____

Take Notes:

Started Date

_____

Finished Date

_____

My Inspiration

_____

_____

_____

_____

_____

_____

My Rating

_____

_____

_____

_____

_____

Book Title:

No.

Author: _____

Publisher: _____

Pages: _____

Book Genre: _____

_____

Started Date

_____

Finished Date

_____

My Review: _____

_____

_____

_____

_____

_____

_____

_____

_____

_____

_____

_____

_____

My Inspiration

_____

_____

_____

_____

_____

_____

_____

My Rating

_____

_____

Take Notes:

_____

_____

_____

_____

Book Title:

No.

Author: _____

Publisher: _____

Pages: _____

Book Genre: _____

_____

My Review: _____

_____

_____

_____

_____

_____

_____

_____

_____

_____

_____

_____

_____

Take Notes:

Started Date

_____

Finished Date

_____

My Inspiration

_____

_____

_____

_____

_____

My Rating

_____

_____

_____

_____

_____

Made in the USA
Coppell, TX
29 May 2020